MY TEACHER & I

A TEACHER AND A STUDENT STORY

DHANANJAY NARAYAN

FOR MY TEACHER,

WHO HELPED ME TO WRITE THIS BOOK.

Contents

Foreword

The team TheRelaxedCat recommends that children should enjoy the book, they should understand the book not just learn the bookish language.They should read as much book as they can and enjoy and understand them.If they understand and enjoy the book their mental abilities will increase.They shouldn't take education as a stress they should take it as a fun.parents should take effort to encourage children till they succeed.Sports, games and arts are as important as education but a better education than better him but if better activities and education than you are the best.

Our goal is to provide better education and creativity and make them understand that all have equal rights to have education and if we get better education and cretivity then our future will be brighter.

Leader

Bihar

Team TheRelaxedCat

27 April 2022

Preface

Dear Readers,

We are happy to present **My Teacher & I**, A great storybook for Indian and International Readers. The texts in the book is fiction and non-fiction. It is a great storybook about a teacher and a student.

Anyone can take any extract from this book to write in their book by author's permission.

We hope that readers find it interesting and useful.

Happy Reading!

Dhananjay Narayan, Amit Ranjan

Acknowledgements

I would like to thank Dr. Amit Ranjan who came up with this idea about this book.

You could contact him at his Youtube Channel (www.youtube.com/c/TheEnglishator)

He is also co-writer of this book. So thanks to him.

And you could know the writer :-

Dhananjay Narayan is new author of the India, The first book he wrote was My Teacher & I that he began writing when he was still in Class 6. He tries to writesbooks in his free time.

You can visit him online at www.therelaxedcat.tk or on E-mail (therelaxedcat007@gmail.com).

And visit co-author at www.youtube.com/c/TheEnglishator

Prologue

In this story, you will read about a teacher and a student.

This story is fiction and also non-fiction.

You will read how they met, how they enjoyed learning, how they get seperated and meet again.

So lets read this amazing story by Dhananjay Narayan of a teacher and a student.

Prologue

[illegible] a teacher and a student.

This story is a [illegible] and also a non-ending.

[illegible] how they met, how [illegible]

[illegible] separated and meet again.

[illegible]

[illegible]

CHAPTER ONE

How We Met

Handshake

I had just shifted from Khagaria and my mom was worried about my studies and looking for a tutor.

And she found a curious teacher and I was confused weather he is a man or woman but he was looking like an early man from stone age because of his long hair and beard.

Also when I discovered he is a man then I was thinking that is he good or bad teacher. I was apprehensive about him.

I discovered that my tutor don't beat kids and is a great follower of Gandhi.

And he had a strange habit of smelling new books because new books smell good.

CHAPTER TWO

Where is God?

Actually my tutor didn't believe that god existed.

At that time, I believed in Gods. My tutor said that there were no gods. And I also started thinking that god never existed after this conversation.

He said "Can you see God?"

Then I said "No"

He said "Can you touch God?"

Then I said "No"

He said "So that proves that there are no Gods."

I said "OK! So that means that there are no brains."

He asked "How?"

I said "Can you see Brain?"

He said "Yes! In photos"

I said "With naked eyes and without photos?"

He said "No"

I said "Can you touch Brain?"

He said "Yes! If I was a doctor"

I said "Your Brain!"

He said "No"

I said "So that proves that no one has brain."

He said "That's not fair."

CHAPTER THREE

Studying Challenges

While teaching me, He gave me some maths problems to solve that he himself couldn't solve.

I could solve those problems but when I couldn't solve it or he solve it faster than me then he said, "Now the camel has come under the mountain".

At that time I was good at maths.

CHAPTER FOUR

Shifting Disaster

After some days, he got shifted to another place and after some days of shifting he stopped teaching me because of extreme heat. And after that my mother found another tutor named Patpata Pandey and he had 2 years of beating experience to beat kids.

CHAPTER FIVE

Patpata got mad

One day, I forgot to do my homework. So he said "Why didn't you did your homework? If you didn't do next time then I will beat you."

After that I obeyed him strictly.

CHAPTER SIX

Unknown guest

Because he beat me we decided to remove him as a tutor.

After removing my tutor Patpata, My mother called Unknown person and I identified that he was my previous tutor who came back in winter.

CHAPTER SEVEN

Tutor looks for a house

When my tutor came back he was in search of a house on rent to live me because he wasn't comfortable in his previous house.

So he asked me for a house nearby and then I asked my mom about it. She recommended my tutor to get a house on rent at Mr. Ken's house.

And my tutor asked for house to Mr. Ken and he agreed to give him a house on rent.

Printed by Libri Plureos GmbH in Hamburg,
Germany